Successful
Team
Building

Successful
Team
Building

Graham Willcocks and Steve Morris

BARRON'S

© Copyright 1997 by Barron's Educational Series, Inc.

First published 1996 in Great Britain by Hodder and Stoughton Educational, copyright © 1995 Graham Willcocks and Steve Morris

All inquiries should be addressed to:
Barron's Educational Series, Inc.
250 Wireless Boulevard
Hauppauge, New York 11788

Library of Congress Catalog Card Number 96-42929

International Standard Book No. 0-7641-0073-4

Library of Congress Cataloging-in-Publication Data
Willcocks, Graham.
    Successful team building / Graham Willcocks and Steve Morris.
        p.   cm. — (Business success series)
    ISBN 0-7641-0073-4
    1. Work groups. I. Morris, Steve, 1962–   . II. Title.
III. Series.
HD66.W534   1997
658.4'02—dc20   96-42929
                                                             CIP

PRINTED IN HONG KONG
98765432

Contents

◆

102797

Introduction

◆

Teams matter—they're an issue on every manager's agenda and in all sorts of articles and journals. They are important in all corners of the manager's world, from the everyday work that goes on no matter what, to the quality and operational initiatives that seem to appear with increasing frequency.

The trouble is that teams are one of those areas that some people assume look after themselves—put a few individuals together, call them a team, and off we go. But a team is like a human being. It is born, grows up, and hopefully reaches maturity. It has its own personality, its own needs and characteristics, and its own pattern of development.

Presumably you wouldn't leave a young child to grow up on his own, without affection, support, and leadership. If you did you could hardly blame anyone else if the person the child grew into turned out to be not exactly what you had hoped. It's the same with teams. They too need support, leadership, and affection. They too need to know the answer to the question children ask most frequently—why?—and get honest answers to other questions that arise. They too need the freedom to establish their role in life, under the guiding hand of someone more experienced.

If they develop well, everybody wins.

This book explores the basic elements that make up successful teams. We will look at why they matter and why they're important—to you, to themselves, and to the organization. We will examine the foundations on which any effective team has to be built, and see how to build on them successfully.

Chapter 1

Why Worry?

This chapter is a brief introduction to the world of teams. There are three questions you need the answers to before you can begin building a successful team. The first one is simply *What are teams and what makes them different from other collections of people?*

The second question is *What's in it for me?* What are the benefits of teams? Why do they matter to the people in them, to me, and to the organization? Is it worth the effort?

The third is *Where do I start?*

Getting positive answers to these questions today will confirm your commitment to making it work.

WHAT MAKES A TEAM A TEAM?

Every Christmas, in thousands of workplaces all over the country, groups of people who happen to work together in the same place go out to lunch. In this group of people are some individuals who don't actually like each other very much, if at all. But they are tolerant of each other throughout the year, because if they didn't the work would suffer and things could get very tense.

Then comes the season of goodwill, and the boss expects these same people to become close friends—just because they have to work next to each other.

However, just putting six or seven people together in the same place to work does not make them a team. It makes them six or seven individuals in the same place.

The same thing happens in committees. If you have ever served on a committee you know that if an issue arises that leads to differences of opinion and causes two or more factions to form, a vote is taken. In mature committees the entire body of the meeting will accept this as the final corporate decision, but in most situations the group that lost the vote will try to sabotage the decision so it fails, and tell everyone outside they didn't agree in the first place.

There is certainly not one team at work here. There may be two— one for each warring faction—but this is a committee. It's not meant to be a team and there are some important differences.

TEAMS ARE SPECIAL

Committees are not set up as teams. Neither are audiences, crowds, or work groups. These are all just collections of people with something in common while they are together, but they aren't working to achieve a common aim. They may discuss common topics of interest or all receive a salary from the same employer, but they do not have to work together.

Committees—especially those in political organizations such as central and local government—are often made up of opposing groups, out to defeat each other. While cynics may say that it sometimes looks as if some sports teams operate in this way—with the defense at odds with the offense—it shouldn't be like that in a team.

CHANGING HATS

The management team in a medium-sized company consisted entirely of individuals who had the dual roles of management team member and head of department. Their management team meetings inevitably turned into a battle for supremacy between the different functions each manager headed—finance, marketing, operations, and so on. They wanted to act more corporately, so they called in a consultant, who sat and watched.

Her first recommendation was to scrap the management team and have head of department meetings, where it was legitimate to battle out budget, status, or resource issues. Later, she said, when they recognized what teamwork really meant, they could reform the management team, and then run both types of meeting.

This example highlights precisely the difference between teams and other groups. Teams have to work together and cooperate to achieve a common aim, while other groups don't.

HORSES FOR COURSES

In most organizations there is room for meetings where

◆ Vested interests can be put forward.

◆ Arguments can be aired for why one department should get more money than another.

◆ The interests of the manager's staff can be protected.

and also for team meetings where

◆ Those present take the wider view and work for the overall success of the organization.

◆ Sectional interests are subordinate to the greater good.

◆ Cross-border issues are explored so departmental and functional barriers do not cloud the issues.

ACTION POINT

Think critically about any teams you're involved in. Are they really teams or are they just groups? Should they be called teams or should someone rename them?

This is by no means as trivial as it might sound. People have expectations of teams and what you call something sets up expectations. If you ask individuals about teams in an organization where the management team is really a collection of departmental heads, they will tell you that the management isn't a team at all.

One tip you might find helpful is simply to call something by the name that reflects its real purpose.

Don't call it a team if it isn't, but if it should be people working together for a common purpose, get the word *team* in there somewhere. It makes a real difference to the expectations people come with and it could make it easier for you to develop a real team approach.

In a team, everybody wins or everybody loses. In a football team you can have someone who hardly touches the ball, but they're still part of a winning team, and if the team loses, they console each other and look forward to getting a better result next time.

You can probably see that there are many underlying characteristics of effective teams. There is also quite a lot of work involved in team building, so before you start that process, let's look at the benefits you can get from teams. After all, why should you bother unless there is something in it for you?

WHAT'S IN IT FOR ME?

How would you justify the job of a manager—what's the purpose? Not what do you do, or what are the separate skills you need, but why are there managers in the first place?

One commonly accepted view is that management is about getting results through other people's performance. That means individuals, groups, and teams.

Imagine trying to get good results at work by dealing only with separate individuals—it just wouldn't work. It would inevitably lead to misunderstandings, different interpretations, a complete breakdown in trust and communication, and very poor personal relationships. You have to work on the team as well as the individuals.

ACTION POINT

Spend a few minutes thinking of any areas where a team is more effective than an individual.

How many of the things under the following headings did you think of? What other things did you come up with?

SOME THINGS NEED SEVERAL SPECIALISTS

Unless one person has all the specialist skills and knowledge you need for a task, it pays to have a team. Of course, if any individual is able to do the whole thing it is worth considering letting them do it. Teams only matter if they make a real difference; there's no point in having them just because they are in fashion.

So, if you have a task or a small project that requires some numerical skills, some practical ability, and report writing talent, collect the individuals with these talents and build a team.

TEAMS REDUCE COMPLEXITY

Imagine you want everyone to help you pack a truck with boxes of goods. If you come to the task without having communicated as a team and worked out who does what, when, and where, and in what order, you are going to have to issue individual and detailed orders as the work proceeds. And, like it or not, it will almost certainly end in chaos and frayed tempers.

In contrast, a team planning the process will almost inevitably sort out all the details with relatively little fuss, and the operation will go smoothly. Even if there are problems, the team will sort them out.

IDEAS TEND TO FLOW

Once you have more than one person thinking about a problem or an issue, ideas start to spark each other off. Someone in the team has experienced a similar problem before, so she has particular knowledge to impart, while someone else has a fresh perspective on it, so she is not limited by past experience.

THE FAMILY AFFAIR

There are emotional benefits in having teams. People start to support and encourage each other, to understand each other better, and to communicate more effectively, even when they are not working together in the team. If someone has a personal problem, it can be made more manageable by talking it over with someone trusted and respected, such as a fellow team member.

It may sound soft, but people need affection and a sense of belonging, even at work. Teams help provide this essential emotional context.

THEY SUPPORT YOUR TRAINING EFFORT

Any new member joining a team will be shown the ropes and helped to make the right moves.

Imagine someone coming to your organization from a similar job elsewhere. If your organization is based on individuals looking after themselves, the others will stand by and watch as the new-comer fills in the wrong documents, does the wrong thing, or gives a wrong answer, because that's what always happens.

In a team, though, someone will quietly come up and assist him, avoiding a potential mess that you'd have to sort out.

DECISIONS TEND TO BE BETTER

No individual knows everything and—as with ideas and knowledge earlier in this list—sharing decisions can identify some solutions you might otherwise not have thought of.

There's another benefit here as well. People, being the emotional animals they are, do not like it if you take a decision and impose it on them—at least some people won't like it. It doesn't matter if it's a sensible decision; what matters is that it's yours, not theirs. This does not mean you have to turn your management role into a democracy, it just means that, where appropriate and relevant, it pays to get the team's involvement in a decision.

Apart from anything else, if they have been involved in the decision, their commitment rockets. Your problem may be stopping them, not getting them going. Even those who aren't entirely convinced are more willing to go along with a decision they had a hand in, and you may find them defending it to others, very unlike the committee arrangements.

WHAT'S IN IT FOR THEM?

So, you know what's in it for you. What about the individuals and the organization?

AS INDIVIDUALS

For the individuals in the team there are benefits of:

◆ greater involvement and empowerment

◆ the chance to play a real part in decision making and implementation

◆ enhanced motivation and greater job satisfaction

◆ more interesting work

◆ the social and emotional benefits seen in the previous list

Can you see anything here that will possibly interfere with your success? Of course not, quite the opposite. Once your people are experiencing these benefits, you will gain with them.

FOR THE ORGANIZATION

Compare two situations, one in an organization where teams are discouraged, and one where they are encouraged.

Which one is going to be the more effective, more successful, and more dynamic?

WHERE DO I START?

Well, you don't just leap into action. The place to start is where you are now, with a clear idea of what teams really are and why they matter. Then recognize that it takes time to build and develop a team.

While you can put a group together in a few minutes, it's important to recognize that teams don't start operating at full power on Day 1. They start off as collections of individuals and they gradually form a coherent team. This is where you come in, as team leader. Your role is to help the team focus on its development and to encourage it to grow into a mature entity, always remembering that you too are one of the team.

This is why this book is shaped as it is, with an introduction in this chapter, a look at the main issues in Chapter 2, and a more detailed look at the key characteristics of teams in Chapters 3 through 6. If you can, wait until you have looked at all the topics before starting to work with the full team on any one of them. Then in Chapter 7 you'll be invited to share your thoughts, knowledge, and ideas with the team, at the start of a team building process.

SUMMARY

In this chapter, we have looked at what exactly teams are. We have examined what benefits they bring to you as a team leader and to the organization and other team members. You are now ready to move into a more detailed exploration of what makes a successful team. We will examine those characteristics in Chapter 2.

Chapter 2

◆

How Your Team
Measures Up Now

In Chapter 1 we looked at why teams are special, what sets them apart from other sorts of groups, and why teams can make all our jobs so much more successful. This chapter will check out what makes special teams special and look at how well one of your teams is doing.

This matters for a very simple but powerful reason. If you are planning to work on improvements to the way your team operates you have to know what improvements are needed. You need to know the following three things:

1. How well *could* the team operate?

2. How is it doing *at the moment?*

3. What are the gaps between how it's doing *now* and how it *could* and *should* be doing?

Only when you know the answers to these questions can you plan the action to bridge the gaps. But you do not do this alone; it is for the whole team to work on.

THE WAY YOUR TEAM COULD WORK

You know that two key issues distinguish teams:

◆ They have a common purpose.

◆ The members of the team have to cooperate and support each other.

These apparently simple statements contain factors that highlight the difference between excellent teams and the rest. Later in the book, we will look at them in more detail.

Shortly, you will compare your team with each factor in turn. You will find that there are some areas where you need to put in more work than others. But first, you need to know what the factors are and what they all mean, at least in outline.

There are six factors in this list:

◆ goals and objectives

◆ the right sort of leadership

◆ complementary skills and roles in the team

◆ an atmosphere of honesty and openness

◆ working methods that flourish in this atmosphere

◆ taking stock of how well individuals and the team are doing

GOALS AND OBJECTIVES

An excellent team has clear, shared goals and objectives. Ask anyone in the team what its purpose is and he or she can tell you.

The question to ask is whether everyone has the same picture of what the team is there for. It may have started out with a clear purpose some time ago—maybe to sort out a particular problem or complete a special project—but is that purpose still valid? Things change over time, so have the goals and objectives altered subtly without being clarified?

If you want people in a team to work together and cooperate for success, they have to know what they are cooperating for. Never assume that everyone else shares your picture of things. Think about your experience as a member of a team and you will almost certainly recall times when you were unsure what you were there to do. Either you never knew because the issue wasn't addressed or the team's goals changed over time.

Whichever it was, the chances are you then invented your own version and operated on guesswork and assumption. You may even have guessed right, but guesswork can never be justified as a sound basis for making plans about an important management activity!

In an excellent team everyone knows the goals because everyone talks about it. Telepathy is not a talent that most of us have, so it is vital that the team's goals and objectives are clear and understood by everyone involved.

THE RIGHT SORT OF LEADERSHIP

> *The effective team leader is part of the team and not someone who stands outside, laying down rules or acting as an autocrat.*

The leader sets the tone. There are teams everywhere in the world of sports and each team has a captain. The captain doesn't just stand around shouting at the other players, he or she plays a full part in what the team does and shares equally in success or failure. He or she listens properly to other team members and gives them support and feedback. The captain is not the only one to congratulate, castigate, or commiserate with other players, and the differences between the leader and the rest just aren't always that obvious to the outsider.

So it is with teams at work. The same sort of issues exist and the way the leader behaves has just as much impact here as it does on a playing field.

COMPLEMENTARY SKILLS AND ROLES

> *An excellent team has all the skills it needs to achieve its purpose and this means having people with different styles, different approaches, and different strengths.*

If you think about what a team does, you can see there are two sides to it.

One side is *what it does*: the activities individuals carry out to get to the objectives. These often include specific skills like planning, selling or making things, and team members carry on doing these when the team is no longer in the same place at the same time. So, the team needs a mix of specific skills.

The other side is *how it does it*: the process the team uses to function properly. The team needs someone to look after its meetings and make sure they are chaired effectively, someone else to sort out details, yet another person to have a broad vision and some bright new ideas. The trouble is that no one person is going to have all these qualities.

AN ATMOSPHERE OF HONESTY AND OPENNESS

> *A hallmark of an excellent team is its members' ability to say what they think or feel, without putting other people down or being put down themselves.*

This one is hard. It cuts across a lot of the normal tendencies people have when they work in organizations. The ideal organization has a culture with no barriers between departments or sections, and is a place where everyone sees themselves as part of the overall team. People serve each other as internal customers and give and receive honest feedback about successes and problems. But too often it really isn't like that.

If you have ever heard people say

◆ "Sorry, that's not my problem."

◆ "Oh, that's the engineer's job . . . nothing to do with me."

◆ "It's the ***!@%! accounts department again!"

◆ "Don't worry about that . . . it's only for the sales people."

then you'll recognize what this means.

The result of a culture like this is that individuals are almost encouraged to try and score points off others. In return they expect to be targeted by them. This leads to an understandable reluctance to say what they really think and an inability to listen without prejudice to what others might say. It's a "watch your back" situation, one where saying nothing means you play it safe in case a fight develops.

You probably don't need any further explanation for now; just imagine how a team would operate if each of the members carried this sort of emotional baggage into the team with them. No trust, no support, and a climate of dishonesty and want to beat the opposition.

WORKING METHODS THAT FLOURISH

An excellent team uses approaches, techniques, and procedures that fit with the right sort of leadership, a climate of honesty and trust, and the acceptance of a range of complementary skills and roles.

It would be a completely pointless exercise to work hard at developing a climate of openness and trust and then for you, the team leader, to storm in and tell the others what they had to do and how.

All the other factors in the list look towards a horizon where:

◆ Each team member matters.

◆ The boss isn't the boss but a fellow team member.

◆ There is mutual trust and support across the team.

This means that the way the team operates—its procedures and conventions—has to reflect this. Procedures have to be in tune rather than discordant. The deeds have to match the words.

Procedures include the way meetings are run, the way decisions are reached, and the approach to handling problems. Any real difference between people's experience of the way the team actually operates on the ground and all the utterances and publicity about what a wonderfully open team it is will show through. Reality will always override slogans.

So, the bottom line is that the procedures have to fit with the culture and values of the team.

TAKING STOCK

> *Excellent teams only stay excellent if they monitor and review what they have done and are doing as a means of continuous improvement.*

It's a simple question to ask, "How are we doing?" but it doesn't get asked enough. You might think it's obvious, but the things under our noses are often the ones we miss. We look out beyond them and forget the basics. In order to stay effective in a changing world we need to ask this question regularly and often.

The answers to the question will generally be about the team as an entity. However, they can also be about individuals who might come up with their own development needs that they want met, in order to play a more effective part in the team.

The only way to do better is to start with how we're doing now. We all learn from experience, as long as we stand still and recognize what the experience means. Someone once said that insanity is doing a second time, with increasing determination, something you have proved doesn't work. But everyone is in danger of making assumptions and jumping into action when the pressure is on and things get really busy.

The alternative takes a little time but it pays dividends, and it is to:

◆ Reflect on what happened.

◆ Identify why it happened.

◆ Plan to repeat the things that worked.

◆ Plan to avoid repeating the things that didn't.

◆ Try out the new approach and start the process again from the top.

HOW IS YOUR TEAM AT PRESENT?

Now that you have confirmed what makes an excellent team, you can check out your own. If you do this on your own you can get a pretty clear picture of the state of things, as long as you:

1. are completely honest;

2. make absolutely no assumptions; if you don't know for sure, don't guess;

3. are confident that everyone else sees things exactly as you do.

You're not sure? Well, for now it's best to stick with your own views. Over the course of the book you will be looking at each factor in more detail, so you could be jumping the gun by starting a wider debate now. Just be aware of these three points as you run through the checklist of how your team is doing.

ACTION POINT

Pick one team that you work with. Ideally, pick one you lead, but if you are still getting ready to build your first team focus on one you are a member of.

Rate the team by selecting the point on the scale where you feel it sits for each of the factors. 1 is very low, or never, and 10 is perfection, or always.

◆

MARK ON A SCALE OF 1–10

◆ Everyone knows exactly what the team's purpose and objectives are.

◆ The leadership style and approach is participatory, not autocratic.

◆ The team members have all the skills and attributes the team needs.

◆ The climate is one where people are always open and honest and don't hold back.

◆ The team meetings and discussions help us operate as a real team.

◆ We regularly ask the question, "How are we doing as a team?"

THE NEXT STEPS

Interpreting the checklist results and identifying a priority order for your team gives you a starting point for action. If you only have two or three issues in need of urgent attention, don't ignore the rest, they still matter and can always be improved, even a little.

My team priorities are:

1.

2.

3.

4.

5.

6.

If you are already leading a team and want to make it even better, then your priority list tells you what you probably suspected, but may not have been able to quantify. The chances are that not everything is a priority. For instance, you may have clear objectives, but a climate where honesty and openness get stifled.

If you are planning to start a team you now have some idea of the main areas to watch out for. In this situation you will have to pay attention to each of the factors as we go through them throughout the book. However, you will have started to sort out for yourself your strengths and weaknesses with regard to leading a team. This insight will help you put your efforts in the right place.

SUMMARY
This chapter looked at how well your team operates *now* and how well it *could* operate. We assessed your team on the basis of its rating on six very important factors, and then prioritized the factors your team needs to improve.

In the following chapter we'll start looking in detail at what action you can take to work on your priorities.

Chapter 3

Follow My Leader

This chapter examines two of the key characteristics of teams: leadership and purpose. Any successful team needs a leader with the skills to hold things together and a clear sense of purpose and direction.

THE TEAM LEADER

The first question to ask is "What makes an effective team leader?" The best way of approaching this is to look at what matters to you when you are on the other side of the fence. What you value will almost certainly match what others value, because human beings are remarkably consistent in this area.

If you think about a team where you were a member and not the leader, it might help you focus on what you valued in the characteristics and skills of the leader. Remember, this is a team, not any other group.

Which of the following do you think makes a more effective leader of a team you're in?

Someone who is totally in control and who

◆ releases just enough information to get things done.

◆ withholds a lot of information and data so he can make the important decisions himself.

◆ tells everyone exactly what they need to do and how to do it.

Someone working in the team as a partner who

◆ shares all available information.

◆ encourages participation and team decision making.

◆ allows people to work out the details themselves.

◆ avoids trying to control everything.

If you look back to Chapter 2, it is fairly obvious that the second set of characteristics is the right set. The first does not fit at all with a team spirit, although it might fit with groups that are not teams.

ACTION POINT

Have a look at the following ten statements and rate yourself as honestly as you can on each one. Give yourself a rating of from 1 (= fair) to 10 (= excellent) for each statement and, if possible, check out your opinion with a friend or colleague who will give you honest feedback on how right she thinks you are.

◆ I know exactly what I want to achieve. ☐

◆ I share my aims and objectives with the rest of the team. ☐

◆ I am loyal to my team and its individual members and I'll defend them if necessary. ☐

◆ I trust the team and its individual members. ☐

◆ I like to delegate in order to help people learn and develop. ☐

◆ I don't duck issues—I face the facts. ☐

◆ I give credit and praise when the team does well, and honest and open feedback with respect when they don't. ☐

◆ I get pleasure and pride from seeing the team and its members do well. ☐

◆ I like to make sure the team has some clear guidelines for its work. ☐

◆ I think work should be enjoyable wherever possible and that job satisfaction is important for everyone. ☐

◆

For most people these are the sorts of characteristics that make up a team leader they really respect and value. In turn, this means that the team members will work their socks off for someone like this, someone they want to do well for out of respect, rather than fear or coercion.

Ten for each one would be nice, but it's unrealistic. You will have some strengths and some weaknesses, so if you allow a range of 6 to 10 as an acceptable level you can start to see where you might need to work on your leadership style. However, even if you scored more than 6 it doesn't mean you are perfect, so avoid complacency. Just work on the biggest needs first.

Start to put together some ideas for a strategy to develop in the areas where you have most room for improvement, and consider sharing the whole issue of your leadership style with the rest of the team, maybe when you're into Chapter 7. After all, they are the ones who will be most affected by the way you operate, so their views can give you valuable information.

MANAGER OR LEADER?

This is an important issue to face. Management can tend to imply control, supervision, and authority. Leadership, however, is based on warmth, honesty, and developing a sense of working together.

There has been a lot of research on the differences between leadership and management and so far no one has clearly cracked the problem. But one way of looking at it is to say that you manage from above, but you can lead from the middle. Management is something that comes in the job description. Leadership is something that other people bestow on you.

If you look around your organization and spot the leaders, you will inevitably find that they are not all the people in control at the top. A leader can be someone on the front line who is adept at getting people to work with her. She could be the person they elected as union representative, because they trust and respect her.

So leaders don't have to be managers, and they often aren't. But managers need to be leaders, if for no other reason than that they have teams to lead rather than manage. Releasing the potential of the other team members is at the heart of any effective team leader's role, and this depends on trust, honesty, openness, and respect, in both directions.

It may be the case that there are some natural-born leaders, who just seem able to get people to follow their lead, apparently without effort. However, most of them have worked at it. To become the sort of leader who can get the best from a team means working on your style and your approach. It means letting go of control and sharing authority, and sharing success and failure too. It isn't easy but once it starts to take off you will be so delighted by the results that it gets easier.

In the list where you looked at the ten characteristics of a leader, a couple were about knowing what you want to achieve and sharing that awareness with the rest of the team. Now that you've started to work on your role, this issue of goals and objectives is the first step in developing the strength of the team.

A SENSE OF DIRECTION

The basic definition of a team we're striving for is individuals working together for a common purpose, so team goals and some clear objectives are important because:

◆ Unless you know where you are going you can't plan and complete the journey.

◆ Without goals and objectives, people will go off in their own direction and the team will split apart as confusion, misunderstanding, and even rivalry grow.

◆ Teams exist even when the team members aren't together. The team does not fade away when a meeting ends; individuals carry on working for the team's goals on their own, so everyone needs to know what their role is and what their tasks are.

THE WRITING TEAM

On the topic of team members working alone at times, this book is one example. The team that produced this book was spread all over the country.

Naturally, there were meetings to get the specification clear and work out who did what, by when, and how team members would support and help each other. So while, for most of the time, the people were not physically close, they did communicate and they were working toward a common goal and some clearly understood objectives.

Having no goals or objectives would be like asking a soccer team to score a goal when there weren't any goal posts and the number of goals that were needed was a secret.

KNOWING WHERE YOU'RE GOING

Most of us have been on a team where we weren't sure of what the team was there for or why it was there because nobody had bothered to wind it up when it had fulfilled its purpose.

One simple way of looking at this issue is to think about meetings you go to, where you are a member of a team rather than its leader.

ACTION POINT

Think about a team you have worked on where there wasn't a clear purpose and consider how it made you feel and how effective it was at getting results.

You probably remember how often you and the other team members groaned about even having to go to meetings because they seemed to have no purpose and achieved nothing. As you shuffled in to meet the rest of the team, you and they probably muttered, "I don't see the point," or "Why are we doing this?" As soon as you get to this level of non-excitement, the team is either dead or in need of resuscitation; it's pointless letting it struggle on in the dark with no commitment.

Now put yourself in the shoes of a team you lead and reflect on how clearly they know what is expected of them. Do not assume they must know just because you do!

If there aren't clear goals for a team to work toward there are two probable reasons:

◆ There simply aren't any goals. Either there never were or there may have been some once, but they have been lost in the mists of time as some of the objectives have been achieved.

◆ Assumptions are being made about what everybody understands.

COMMON PURPOSE

Before the start of your next team meeting write down on a piece of paper what you see as the purpose of the team—what it is there to achieve. Then at the start of the meeting get the other team members to write down their versions, on their own, and afterwards compare the results. The similarity or difference will give you something very valuable to discuss when you get to Chapter 7 and you open up the debate with the rest of the team.

If there is any doubt or confusion, the responsibility for clarifying goals rests with you. You don't have to sort out all the details, but it is the team leader's job to make sure that everyone is working for the same broad goals. However, don't invent goals for the sake of it. If the team was set up to do something it has completed, wrap it up with a celebration and concentrate on teams with something important left to do.

GOALS AND OBJECTIVES

While you know it is important to let the team make decisions and to plan its own operations as far as possible, it is you who decides to set up a team in the first place because there is something you think it can do. At the very start you know what this is and they don't.

ACTION POINT

Think of a team you set up fairly recently. What was the goal? What did you want it to achieve?

This goal is the broad target you set, probably even before you picked the people you thought would make the right team. So the first issue to sort out when you have everyone in the same room—assuming they know each other and don't need much introduction—is why they are there.

The reason we are working as a team is that we need to . . .

Stop there. Let it sink in and make sure everyone has the same clear picture of what the future will look like when you have achieved the goal.

Then start to turn it over to them. Ask a question and sit back.

How do you think we could go about this?

Once the discussion gets going, some steps to success will start to emerge.

Well, we need to get the paperwork organized.

Yes, and the accounting department needs to know what we're up to, because it affects them.

Perhaps the main thing is to get the locations for the machines sorted out and arrange the power supply.

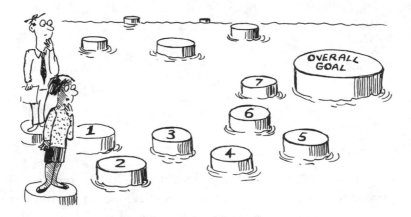

Whatever emerges can be turned into objectives—more detailed steps along the way to the overall goal. Objectives are an essential starting point, often written so they say:

The objective is to . . . [specify exactly what is to be done] . . . *by* . . . [whenever it is needed].

However, you may need a bit more than the bare objective. Have you ever been to a meeting where an argument started when you asked Bill how something was going—thinking Bill was handling it—and Bill says it had been a job that Jim had said he'd handle? Jim recalls quite distinctly that it had been given to Joyce, who claims to know nothing about it. If you have, you will know that it is a time-consuming waste of energy.

Whether individuals or sub-teams from the big team are going to tackle certain steps, there has to be some way of ensuring that everyone knows what they and everyone else is doing, and what the constraints—deadlines, resource limits, and so on—are. There are some simple words that can help here:

◆ What?

◆ Why?

◆ Who?

◆ How?

◆ Where?

◆ When?

Consider constructing a simple form with these words on it, so that for each of the steps along the way, for each objective, you can specify as a team exactly what is to be achieved and by when. Not only does it avoid confusion at the start, it also gives you something to use as a measure as progress unfolds. If one key objective is slipping you can focus on it when you review progress and take corrective action.

SUMMARY

By the end of this chapter you have probably made a start on two of the key issues in teams: your leadership, and the direction the team is heading in. You won't have sorted everything out yet, but remember that Chapter 7 is reserved for putting all the issues together and reviewing where you stand.

In the next chapter, you will look at another key issue: what role you want other people to play in the team, so they carry their share of the weight and support you in your job of leading.

Chapter 4

The Sum of the Parts

This chapter explores the roles individuals play in the team—not only their specialist roles but their roles as team players as well. A team is not just a number of individuals. It's a machine operating as a complete entity, using a range of components and parts. In the team, these components are people.

Think about a bicycle. It needs all its different components in order to work: wheels, pedals, a frame, handlebars, and so on. Some components look shiny and some, like the saddle, should make you feel comfortable. The chain, however, is probably greasy, and you don't really like getting your hands on it. But you can't operate effectively without a chain.

Team composition is the same. There will be some people who play a part you are very comfortable with, and others you find difficult to handle, who make you feel uncomfortable. There are two sides to this in teams:

◆ The right technical mix of skills, **what** the people do as specialists

◆ The right mix of team skills, **how** they operate to add value to the team

THE RIGHT TECHNICAL MIX

This is a relatively straightforward issue. It comes down to having specialist skills in place to cover the technical tasks that have to be completed en route to achieving the goal.

ACTION POINT

If you were setting up a team to turn the garbage dump at the main office into a garden, what sort of technical skills would you want people to bring to the team?

◆

You would probably want to include individuals who knew about:

◆ horticulture, so you could use their expertise on what to plant where, and to ensure the right soil conditions;

◆ plant and machinery, so that any excavation could be handled by someone who knew which machines to use and how to operate them;

◆ electricity and wiring, to handle the power supply to the lights and the fountain;

◆ plumbing, to figure out the water supply;

◆ finance, to help keep an eye on the costs against the budget.

All these people may not be available, though, so you would have to compromise and find the best mix of skills you could. Maybe you don't have access to specialist trades like machinery, electrical contracting and plumbing, in which case you may get someone with experience in selecting and managing outside contractors. Whatever you end up with, the mix will be as appropriate as you can get it.

IT DOESN'T STOP THERE

So, you have six or seven people with specialist skills in the same place at the same time. Are they a team? Not yet, this is where you started, in Chapter 1.

What makes them a team? Working together for a common purpose—the basic definition again. You need the individuals you selected to take a wider view of the whole project and share

ownership of the overall goal. Each one is not there just because they can drive a bulldozer, make a watertight joint, or add up figures. They are there to add something else—the magic that turns them into a team.

BASEBALL MANAGING

A veteran baseball manager who had come up through the ranks was once asked about the differences in coaching an all-star team and his regular season team.

He replied that while the individual players on his league team were not necessarily the best in the league at their assigned positions, they did know each other and worked on strategies together. They understood almost instinctively what each of their fellow players would do in a certain situation. This team dimension added to the skills they already had. There was no room for a star who didn't fit in with the team.

At the all-star level, although he worked with the best players in the league, they had only a few days together and it was infinitely harder to get that extra magic that meant they functioned as a real team.

So, back to the garden team. If you give them the goal—to get a garden built within six months inside a budget of $XX—and then turn them loose to sort out the objectives, the chances are they will all pick up their natural technical roles automatically. The finance person won't ask someone else to handle the figures while they drive the bulldozer, and the horticulturist won't suggest someone else looks after the planting because they want to do the wiring. They know what to do.

So the *what* of the team roles looks after itself, if you choose the people correctly. The *how* needs a little bit more attention.

THE RIGHT TEAM MIX

The issue here is what individual team members do to help the team achieve success. What difference does their behavior and their approach make to the way the team operates?

If you had the chance to appoint someone as your assistant, would you choose someone exactly like you or someone different? Why?

Many people choose people who are like them to work with, cloning themselves. It makes life comfortable and means there is always someone else who sees things from the same sort of perspective, but it isn't the best approach. You end up with two people doing the same things and nobody filling in the gaps.

If you choose someone different you could select someone who would

◆ do the things you didn't like.

◆ fill in the gaps where you were not entirely competent and confident.

◆ complement you in the things you were good at.

◆ have his own role rather than duplicate yours.

◆ bring another perspective to ideas and decisions.

Nobody can be good at everything. You don't see sports teams where the players are interchangeable, equally skilled at defense and offense.

An effective team is made up of individuals with their own strengths and weaknesses. The secret is to put together a team that has all the potential weaknesses covered somewhere, so you have a full range of strengths. By definition this means avoiding cloning, making sure that there are some very different characters in the team who may not feel comfortable with each other at first.

As leader, it is important that you pick people—or develop the roles of those already in the team—who match up with some classic characteristics that make for an effective and rounded team. There is a cast of characters who together make up a well-rounded team.

THE CREATIVE THINKER

This individual comes up with some weird and wonderful ideas, sometimes when you're in the middle of something else! Their brain always seems to be on the lookout for other ways of doing things. They aren't always very good at making their ideas work and figuring out the details, but where would the team be without ideas and sharp flashes of insight?

THE ACTION PERSON

Here is someone who never comes up with a new idea but takes someone else's idea and turns it into reality. They quietly work away on the details and make sure it gets done. Their character means they need to know what the outcome might look like before they start work, but once they're off they will do a great deal of the work, or make sure it gets done. Clearly, this individual is very different from the creative thinker, but they work very well together as long as they are on the same team and working toward the same ends.

THE PUSHER

This is the person who looks at her watch and reminds you there's only half an hour left and still a lot to do. They push for action and don't really like all that thinking and planning. This is helpful because it can keep the momentum going, but it can be annoying to the other team members who relish the detail and the creative process for its own sake.

THE SCRUTINEER

In the middle of an exciting discussion about how an objective can be achieved, the scrutineer looks up from the data and says you can't afford it, or it would mean more work elsewhere because of the domino effect. These people bring you down to earth with a bump by always having their feet firmly on the ground and coming up with the practicalities, problems, and difficulties. This can be extremely difficult if you are a creative thinker, but it does stop the team from going down paths of fantasy.

THE SMOOTHER

This is generally someone who hates conflict and argument, so they try and mediate between opposing factions and find some common ground. Smoothers really care about the people on the team and work hard to make sure everyone feels all right, even when it is unrealistic. However, they act as a sort of mirror that reminds everyone to stay civilized, and in doing so, perform a very valuable function for the team as a whole.

THE STINGER

This is someone everybody thinks at times is rude, abrasive, and awkward. Stingers confront other people directly and come up with all sorts of moral and practical arguments to explain why they would do things differently. They liven up team meetings and get the adrenaline flowing, which in itself is a valuable alternative to just drifting along with the tide of opinion. In doing so, they can offend, irritate, and intimidate their colleagues, but their contribution is often extremely sensible. However, it can get ignored because the other people don't listen to what is being said, they're too busy getting angry with the stinger.

THE CONDUCTOR

Here is the person who keeps time and ensures everyone is in tune, managing the process of team meetings and making sure people have the chance to speak and be heard. He or she watches the way things are going and reflects what has been said. They summarize from time to time and act like an effective chairperson in a meeting. Without this, individual meetings may never achieve their purpose and the quieter individuals such as the scrutineer, may never get a word in edgewise and may give up trying.

ACTION POINT

Write down the names of the people on a team you lead. In your mind, picture them and the way they behave and decide which of the preceding types each most closely resembles.

Hopefully you have a fair spread. You need neither too many of one type or none of another, because if you have the wrong mix there will be some weaknesses left and too much strength in other areas. The team won't balance.

The problem is that you may not have had the chance to pick the team—you work with what is there. This means that you may need to discuss team roles with the individuals concerned and find out whether there are hidden talents you can draw on to fill any of the gaps. One important facet of this is to open up the whole issue and help the other team members to see that just because someone else does not behave as they do, it does not make them a bad team player.

This is especially crucial with some of the characters. For example, getting everyone to see that the stinger is not just a darn nuisance but someone who benefits the team isn't always easy, but it is worth the effort. You could give them the descriptions of the cast of characters and get them to say how they see their team. It starts them talking about the issues and helps weld the team together.

And, if someone else turns out to be a better conductor than you are, how about letting them chair some meetings? This is perhaps too radical a suggestion for many people, because the chair is tradition-ally associated with the person with the greatest authority. However, if your natural approach is to be a creative thinker or a pusher then the chances are you and the team will lose out in two ways:

1. It's harder to manage the process effectively and you won't get the best from the rest of the team; the results the conductor should get just won't appear.

2. The natural talents you do have will be lost or diluted as you try to fit into a role that you don't like, while someone who is a nat-ural is sitting there trying to do a different job or just opting out.

DEALING WITH WEAK TEAM MEMBERS

You may be appointed leader of a team that already exists, or you may have to choose your team from a limited pool of workers. In these circumstances it is not unusual for the team to have some weak team members who can adversely affect the performance of the team as a whole. The weaknesses can include limitations in job skills or team skills, or they may have some personal or emotional problems that render them unsuitable for teamwork.

In most cases, a caring and supportive team can strengthen weak team members so that it is not necessary to replace them. One problem with immediately deciding to replace weak team members is that there is no guarantee that the replacement members will not bring other problems to the team. However, if you have a team member that lacks the critical job skill that it is intended she brings to the team (for example, the aerodynamicist in an aircraft design project team, the anaesthesiologist in a surgical team), replacement may be the most efficient solution to the problem.

Other techniques can be implemented by the team to strengthen weak team members:

1. Set up a series of formal presentations in which each team member describes to the remainder of the team what their particular skills can bring to the team project. Follow this with an open discussion about the presentation and how the particular skill can help accomplish the team's goals. In preparation for the presentation the weak team member will be forced to carefully review how his skills benefit the team. A tremendous amount of study will be accomplished in the process thereby strengthening his skills and capability as it relates to the project. You may offer your assistance to the weak team member in this presentation preparation. This process will give him the opportunity to discuss his contribution, an opportunity that might not otherwise occur. In addition, the open discussions that follow the presentation involve the weak team member in effective team communication.

2. You should spend some time with each weak team member and have project-related discussions with them. It sometimes helps to have these with the weak team member and her operational superior. During these meetings the member's boss may recognize the weakness and provide training and support to strengthen the

team member. It may also help you as team leader, because if the weak team member cannot provide the service you need, the member's boss may recommend a better replacement team member, thereby solving your problem.

DEALING WITH DIFFICULT TEAM MEMBERS

Sometimes two team members may have what appear to be irreconcilable differences, which are causing severe team disruption and short circuiting other team achievements. In such cases it may be best to remove one of the two individuals (or in the worst case, both individuals) from the team. The team leader should consider replaceability and compatability with the rest of the team in making the decision to remove one or both of the team members.

If the team leader decides that the differences between the team members can be resolved, a number of strategies can help to resolve those differences:

1. If you have the time, arrange a social event such as a picnic or dinner for the team and try to plan it so that the incompatible team members are seated close to each other. Encourage conversation about non-work-related topics, family matters, hobbies, automobiles, houses, and so on. Often you will find that the two team members have something in common in one or more of these non-work subjects and that their conversation will begin to break down barriers or differences. They will find each other to be in some ways more compatible than they had previously imagined and this will help their work relationship.

2. Plan a team survival course in which all team members at one time or another totally depend on each other for their safety. This has the overall effect of introducing a high level of trust among

all the team members, including those who seem incompatible. Preplanned courses or activities are available through specialized management consultants.

3. Have a personal talk with each of the difficult team members and attempt to discover the root cause of their incompatability. Sometimes these are issues that you as team leader can help resolve.

SUMMARY

The roles team members play are complex. We have seen that the makeup of the team is not just a simple matter of gathering the right number of people together. Rather, it depends on the right mix of skills, behavior, and approach, and an awareness of the importance of the other people's roles across the whole team. Behind it all is your leadership role, encouraging this whole area of differences to be seen as a benefit and not a blockage to progress.

Chapter 5

To Be Honest

Remember what you read in Chapter 2?

> *A hallmark of an excellent team is its members' ability to say what they think or feel, without putting other people down or being put down themselves.*

TEAMS ARE PEOPLE, AND PEOPLE ARE EMOTIONAL

When teams are working at peak performance they are emotional entities. They need to operate in a climate of mutual support and trust, so that even if two team members hold opposing views, they don't allow the disagreement to become personal. In the same way, if one member feels upset or disappointed about something a colleague has done, he needs to be able to say what he thinks or feels and expect to be heard. No one else may agree with him, but the open exchange of views, opinions, values, and ideas is healthy and constructive.

For individuals to make a worthwhile contribution they have to feel valued and listened to, even if they don't always get their own way. They have to feel other people want to hear from them.

ACTION POINT

Think about a meeting you have been at, where someone either sneered at an idea you put forward or simply ignored you. Maybe you tried to put your point across and someone else just talked over you. How did that make you feel about yourself, the rest of the team, and your future role?

◆

The chances are you felt some extreme emotions: anger, resentment, frustration, and a desire to get even. Or else you sighed sadly and gave up. Neither of these is at all helpful when it comes to a successful team, because the next natural reaction is to come away and promise yourself you'll keep quiet next time, or you'll get even. But you're not alone in feeling like this. Everyone else does as well, especially characters like the smoother, the action person, and the scrutineer.

THE COMMUNICATION TRAP

Without a climate of trust and respect, individuals can fall into the communication trap and stop communicating effectively as instead they:

◆ hold back from making contributions, so they feel frustrated and left out, and the whole team misses out on their ideas and views

◆ sit on emotions that eat away at them afterwards, leading to mutual dislike and mistrust that shows up in deliberate actions and negative body language

◆ go their own way and plan secret approaches at odds with what the rest of the team is aiming for

The bottom line is that if this happens, dissatisfaction starts to spread and real issues get buried. Helping them avoid the communication trap makes people feel warm and comfortable. Only if they feel good about themselves and the contribution they make will they act as a team, not just a group.

Here's an important tip: Always try, like the manager in the next example, to work on team building at the start of the team's life. It allows you to encourage good habits instead of having to undo existing bad ones, which are often deeply rooted and hard to shift.

SHIPWRECKED!

The marketing manager in a small packaging firm was setting up a small project team. They all knew each other from a previous project, which hadn't gone very smoothly. The marketing manager asked the head of personnel and training to sit in on the first meeting and give them some tips to help develop the team approach.

The head of personnel used the first hour of their meeting for an exercise—a scenario where the team was supposed to have been shipwrecked and had to work together on an escape strategy. When he gave his feedback on what had happened and why they had come up with a strategy that meant they were all dead, he made the following observations.

First, he said, the team balance was way off: three pushers, one smoother, a creative thinker—who happened to be the marketing manager—and a stinger. No one acted as conductor and managed the process.

The pushers had tried to take control and had jostled for supremacy, hogging the discussion and blocking anyone else, especially the quieter types, from making their points. The stinger hadn't joined in at all.

The pushers said if the others wanted to say anything they should have, which angered the quieter ones. They said they had tried to make a contribution but were always ignored, told to hang on a minute, or were told they were wrong. So they gave up, leaned back in their chairs, and withdrew. The stinger just said it was a shambles and he wanted nothing to do with it. Some increasingly personal and hurtful comments were thrown around: "You never listen anyway—you're just a bully," and "People like you have to be led by someone strong like me, or you'd never figure it out."

◆

Now, the important issue in this example is not whether the team concerned got the right answer. As it happens they didn't, which tells you something about the way they operated. They could always have come up with the right answer by mistake, but that's no way to run an effective team. What really matters is the way they behaved with each other. They were meant to be on the same side, working together to save themselves and their colleagues from a watery grave. Instead, they fell straight into the communication trap.

━━━━━━━━━━━━━━━━━◆━━━━━━━━━━━━━━━━━

ACTION POINT

Ask yourself, does this example ring any bells with you, from your experience? If it does, think about how people's behavior needs to change if they are to operate properly as a team.

◆

The answer is simple: they need to avoid doing all the things that lead to the communication trap. This means they have to stick to the points in the following checklist.

CHECKLIST FOR AVOIDING THE COMMUNICATION TRAP

◆ Listen to other people's contributions. Remember, listening is an active process, it isn't the same as waiting for your turn to speak.

◆ Accept that you aren't the only one with feelings who gets hurt—everyone does, so put yourself in their shoes and don't make disagreements personal.

◆ Recognize the importance of all the other team members and the roles they play. Accept that a stinger is making a positive contribution and accept that a quiet individual may need encouragement to speak her mind.

◆ Deal with the facts, not the individual. If you disagree with a point of view say, "I disagree with the point of view," not "That's stupid."

◆ Respond, don't react. Think for a couple of seconds before you launch into a personal counterattack, especially when it is someone whose team role is very different from yours.

◆

However, making this happen isn't so simple. The team needs to go through some key steps if every member is going to communicate effectively and avoid the communication trap.

A FOUR-STEP APPROACH TO MAKING IT HAPPEN
The steps needed to make it happen are these:

1. Gain acceptance from everyone that there are potential dangers or room for improvement.

2. Make everyone responsible for their actions in solving the problem or stopping one from developing.

3. Identify and agree on some ground rules for fair play.

4. Make sure everyone sticks to the rules, and remind them if they don't.

USING ALL FOUR STEPS
You have to cover all four points. It is vital that everyone understands exactly what the dangers are and shares ownership of the issue. Then, when they work out ways of preventing problems, it is *their* solution to *their* problem in *their* team and they will all have a stake in making it work. Try and impose *your* solution and it won't stick, even if it happens to be the same solution they come up with! It's simple psychology, but it is important.

STEPS 1 AND 2

To cover steps 1 and 2 you could, either on your own or with the support of the people who manage your training:

◆ Explain the issue of openness, honesty, and trust in teams, as it is set out in this book, to set the scene.

◆ Give the team a simulated task to do. There are lots of them available commercially or you could devise your own, such as redesign the car parking or plan a new form or a new system.

◆ Ideally, you should videotape the exercise, or get one of the team members to sit outside the team and watch what happens, using the checklist to assess how things go.

◆ Make key notes on a board as you ask people at the end individually:
  – what happened
  – how they feel and felt, emotionally, and why
  – what they think went well
  – what they think went badly

◆ Either play the video or get feedback from the observer and confirm the points everyone feels could be improved.

It is guaranteed that there will be several things that do go well, and these are important. If you start feedback by saying what went well, people are far more ready to hear about what didn't.

It's also guaranteed that there will be things that go wrong—examples of the communication trap. By identifying these themselves, the team—including you—will draw up their own agenda of things to be tackled.

STEP 3

Remember the tip about getting team building going at the start of the team's life? Well, here it is important because it lets the team sort out and clarify some ground rules before they get into detailed and possibly heated discussion on real and important tasks.

You need to let the team draw up its own ground rules, but you could start by giving them guidelines. The following is one set of rights and responsibilities that you could use to get the ball rolling:

Everyone on this team has the right to:

◆ express views and opinions, however unpopular

◆ be listened to without interruption and with respect

◆ say no or yes without feeling guilty

◆ change his or her mind

◆ say "I don't know" or "I don't understand"

Everyone on this team has a responsibility to:

◆ accept that other people are different but equal

◆ behave appropriately

◆ look for strengths, not weaknesses in other people

◆ listen to others' opinions with an open mind

◆ avoid causing emotional injury or hurt

Compiling a similar set of rights and responsibilities is one way to clarify ground rules.

Another approach is to describe what is required behavior, so the list could be along the lines of:

◆ When one person is talking, all others must listen until he has finished.

◆ Someone wanting to make a contribution must be allowed to do so, without someone else jumping in.

◆ When speaking, say "I feel" or "I think," rather than "We feel" or "That is," because it focuses the speaker and helps her make sure she says what she really means.

Once the ground rules have been established and agreed on by everybody, you have a set of working guidelines that can be applied, monitored, and policed.

STEP 4

Enforcing rules is done at two levels: the immediate and the reflective. The immediate level may be in a team meeting where the conductor—you or whoever it is—has to watch the process and stop someone from breaking the rules. In meetings it can be a simple matter of saying something like:

Pat, hang on a minute, Lynn hasn't finished.

Pat, hang on a minute. Lynn, you looked like you were going to say something.

Because you are enforcing everybody's rules, there will be no animosity and very little argument.

The reflective level is where you use some of the techniques from Steps 1 and 2, reviewing what happened and continuing to learn and improve the way things are done. (This is the whole point of Chapter 7's look at reviewing.)

Like all the other characteristics, the one you have looked at in this chapter doesn't happen in one attempt. It takes time and effort, especially if your organization doesn't normally work this way.

THE CULTURAL PULL

What if you are trying to set up an open, honest, and trusting team, in an organization where this is just not the way it works? What if the organization has huge departmental barriers and there is a culture of blame and unhealthy competition, the sort of culture where the management team is really a battleground for heads of department? Perhaps you hear comments such as:

Don't tell them the whole story or they'll know as much as we do.

We stiffed the others in that meeting—I got their budget reduced and ours increased.

Send a memo—just to cover your back!

ACTION POINT

If your work environment feels anything like one where you might hear talk like this, think about how it affects your team, especially if the team is made up of individuals from different parts of the organization.

◆

Perhaps the key thing is that the people in the team will naturally be more suspicious of an open and honest approach if they are not used to this sort of culture. It might take a little more time to get everybody to trust everybody else. The bottom line, though, is that you should only bother to try and change things you have a chance of changing. And remember, you alone will not change the organization's culture.

However, you can change the behavior of your team members, so once you start making progress, forget the culture. Somewhere, at some time, what you achieve in your team will be held up as a model of what can be done with the right approach, and then you will have done your bit to change the rest of the world.

EXAMPLES OF RIGHT AND WRONG APPROACHES

Image that your team is responsible for designing, manufacturing, and delivering large sections of an aircraft to an aircraft manufacturer. The quality of the hardware being produced in your plant is being criticized by your customer and government inspectors. You are late in your deliveries by four weeks, and things are getting worse. In addition, your costs are increasing and are already way over your selling price. What to do?

WRONG SOLUTION:

You gather the team together in a room and berate them for their poor performance. You tell them they are incompetent, lazy, they don't know what they are doing, and if they don't shape up you will personally see to it that they are replaced with members that do know what they are doing. You set quality and delivery targets that they must meet to bring the project under control. You will not listen to them because they failed you, and only you know the right answers.

This nonsolution will inevitably lead to acrimony among the team members, chaos in the production line, and no improvement in your quality and delivery situation. You have not helped them or yourself understand why the situation is the way it is, what are the root causes of the problems, and how they can be fixed. You have merely told them to go and find their own solutions, and that their jobs are in jeopardy if they don't succeed. The team members begin to function as isolated, fearful individuals, quick to point fingers at others, whose only solution is to work harder and longer at doing what they were doing before, hoping that will improve the situation and save their jobs.

RIGHT SOLUTION:

Bring the team together and review with them in some detail the specifics of the quality, cost, and delivery problems the team is faced with. Ask each team member to share with the rest of the team what he or she thinks are causing these problems. Then ask them, if there were no constraints, what they would do to fix them. Encourage them to be honest, to say exactly what they think the causes of the problems really are.

Foster an atmosphere in which finger pointing and personal attacks are discouraged, and where a more objective approach is prevalent.

In turn ask the other team members what they think the problems and solutions are. This should be followed by an open discussion. Then create a list of team-generated actions that the team believes will solve the quality, cost, and delivery problems. Team members should be encouraged to volunteer responsibility for each action, and if there are no volunteers for certain items, you should take the action. Each team member with self-assigned actions is invited to set a schedule for completion of each. As the team leader, you must ensure that all of these scheduled actions lead to a timely resolution of the project problems.

As you demonstrate to the team how critical each person's actions are to the timely overall solution, you will find that they will adjust their schedules to support the on-time completion of the project. You will also find that since these actions are the result of the team's own assessment of the root causes of the problems, they will take full ownership and responsibility for the successful accomplishment of their actions, and you will have developed the maximum capability of your team. You must also be prepared to take certain actions, particularly those that are outside the team's control but are necessary for the resolution of the problems.

SUMMARY

In this chapter, we have considered the people in the team. There are many potential pitfalls when different personalities are put together, but with careful preparation these can be avoided and personality clashes avoided. To do this we set out a four stage process which will help avoid the communication trap.

Not only do individual personalities create difficulties but the personality of the organization might be a problem too. Remember, you might not be able to change the organization's culture overnight, but developing your team culture could be the first step along the way.

This issue of openness, honesty, trust and respect is perhaps the hardest of all to crack, simply because it is about personal communication and everyone thinks they communicate pretty well. This is often reinforced in the way procedures are set up, which is the topic for Chapter 6.

Chapter 6

It's Not What
You Do

So far you have established that teams are special and that they:

◆ depend on effective leadership and clear goals

◆ bring together a blend of some very different skills

◆ need people to communicate openly and honestly

This chapter focuses on an issue that builds on all these things—the way the team works to achieve its goals and objectives through discussion and decision-making procedures. It's a practical lesson, full of ideas and activities you can use to develop procedures that work best in your team.

It is important to establish ways of operating that fit the team and make use of all the work you have done so far, using their joint potential and enhancing the way each member is going to be involved and play a full part. It's also important to make sure they don't all look to you, their team leader, every time there is a decision to be made, or when the team needs to plan its next steps. Appropriate procedures involve everyone in ideas, information, and decisions. The three techniques explained here can help start that process off.

People work best when they feel enthusiastic about the process, and to work effectively, any procedure in a team should not only be worthwhile, it should be satisfying, even fun, and you can prove this if you try out the following team techniques as party games. They work just as well.

TWO OR MORE HEADS ARE BETTER THAN ONE

One of the benefits of teams is that ideas tend to flow, as one person sparks off another. Having put together a team:

◆ with the right mix of skills

◆ that knows what its job is

◆ where you provide effective leadership from the middle of the team rather than as a boss

◆ with people communicating openly and honestly

you have all the components for a technique called brainstorming, which can give you an excellent range of ideas. It also works when you are trying to find all the possible causes of a difficulty, or are looking for solutions to problems.

BRAINSTORMING

Brainstorming is a technique that helps break down the restrictive approach to thinking that much of the educational system and many management techniques aim for: the search for a single right answer. Often there are several possible answers and before you decide on which one is right for your situation, you have to get as many of the possibilities out in the open as you can.

Sometimes brainstorming is thought to be just a group of people throwing ideas around, but when it is done properly there are some rules to it that make it a really creative approach.

BRAINSTORMING RULES

Specify clearly a problem or a question and make sure it is understood in the same way by everyone. Then you need one person to stand at a flip chart or whiteboard and act as recorder and controller. His primary job is to write down what everyone says, without changing it in any way; even if two people say almost the same thing, write them both down. His other job is to enforce the rules that follow.

PHASE 1

People call out their ideas, which can be as wacky as they like.

Nobody is allowed to criticize or praise what someone else has said, it goes down exactly as called out without any evaluation of its suitability or feasibility. (This is an important rule for the recorder to enforce.)

Whatever is called out gets written down, *verbatim*.

PHASE 2

At the end of the first phase you have line after line of ideas on the board. The recorder leads the team in grouping together any ideas with a common thread; in the paper clip example that follows shortly, there would be all those that use the clip as a tool, for instance.

PHASE 3

The team then goes through and agrees which ideas are completely unrealistic, and they get crossed off. The remaining ideas are then discussed and evaluated using whatever criteria the team sets for the task. You end up with a range of possible ideas that then can be refined into one or two workable options.

Any ideas produced in this way come from the team, are owned by the team, and harness every scrap of creative thinking that exists.

ACTION POINT

Get the rules very clear in your mind, so tomorrow you can try it out with your team, using this common example: what uses are there for a paper clip?

The results can be quite astounding, as you'll see when you try it. The creativity triggered by being encouraged to think outside the normal "sensible" boundaries at work or by one person sparking off a related idea in someone else can be really useful in what it produces. However, more importantly, it puts the creative emphasis on the whole team and gets them involved right at the center.

Another approach that helps people to share the information and knowledge they have—and sometimes don't even realize they have—is a technique we'll call collage, because it builds up a picture from various scraps of material.

COLLAGE

This is a procedure with two stages, individual and team. You can use just the second stage, but it really adds worthwhile thinking time if you build in stage 1 as well.

COLLAGE RULES

1. Put together 10 factual questions on a topic everybody knows something about, pop music in the '80s or Health and Safety rules, for instance.

2. Try and make a few of the questions multipart, so the team members might get some parts right but not all.

3. Prepare a question sheet for each team member and an answer sheet, to use later.

4. Get individuals to tackle the questions alone, with no conferring at all, within a reasonable time limit.

5. Then, in a longer time period (as discussion takes longer) get them to come up with answers the whole team accepts.

6. Finally, give them the answers so they can check their individual answers and the team's answers. Be strict about marking; they must be right or score nothing.

Invariably, the team gets far more right than any individual, except in the unusual event of someone being an expert on the topic. If you ask the team what this shows they will say things like:

We get better answers when we pool our knowledge.

What so-and-so said was nearly right, and it triggered the right answer in my brain.

I don't mind sharing what I know with them; it works both ways.

ACTION POINT

Start working on some questions and answers so you can use the technique tomorrow with the team.

Collage helps narrow down all the available information in people's heads and add it to what other people know. It can produce remarkable results.

I NEVER WOULD HAVE GUESSED . . .

A team of taxi drivers using this technique worked on questions about traffic law. On the team was the 17-year-old daughter of the firm's owner, who ran the radio.

The drivers clearly thought she wouldn't get many right and they looked a bit smug, even patronizing. But when the questions were marked her individual score was the highest, and all the drivers admitted that she had played the major part in helping the team get a high score. They said it had been an eye-opener. Never assume someone can't make a really valuable contribution.

While the drivers had forgotten much of what they knew, the girl who ran the radio was about to take her driving test, so she had been boning up on the information.

Facts and decisions are likely to be of a higher quality when teams use collage, because more people are making contributions and adding information from their own knowledge and experience.

Sometimes, though, a right answer is obscured because it's buried somewhere under a mass of irrelevant and trivial detail. A team technique for helping with this issue is one we call information overload.

INFORMATION OVERLOAD

Using this technique not only allows the team to look at how information is passed around, it also provides the opportunity to look at issues like the communication trap.

You can draw up your own example, but to save you time, one has been put together for you to use, if you prefer. It is designed ideally for seven people, so they have three pieces of information each. If you have eight or nine in your team you could give a few people two pieces of information or you could get a couple of the team members to act as observers and give feedback on how the process went, at the end.

If you have fewer than seven, give out extra pieces of information to team members. They should all have roughly the same number of cards.

Because you know what is happening, you need to stay out of this activity.

INFORMATION OVERLOAD RULES

Type (or print) the following statement to give to everyone in the team.

> *At 6:00 P.M. on Tuesday, March 4, 68 people left their homes in town to go to a leisure activity. How many went to see the hypnotist?*

Now write the separate pieces of information shown on separate cards.

To start the activity, mix up the cards so they are entirely random and give them out to the team. Their task is to answer the question in the statement they received. You do nothing else.

The only leisure activities on Tuesdays are baseball practice, karate, and anything on at the Town Hall.	Tuesday evening is training night for the town's baseball team and their two reserves.
Jones is a builder, with a pick-up truck.	There is a talk at the Town Hall tonight.
The Sports Bar is five hundred yards from the Town Hall.	All events at the Town Hall start promptly at 7:00.
The Rovers' coach lives in the town.	The baseball team faces relegation.
The Town Hall was built in 1923 from charitable donations.	The Karate Club is preparing for an international competition.
The three who went to the bar left together at 6:45.	The baseball coach played for Arsenal, years ago.
The Town Hall speaker is a hypnotist.	The hypnotist has three grandchildren.
No hypnotists live in the town.	Hypnotism is an ancient art.
Smith and King never miss their Tuesday Karate Club at 7:15.	Jones, King, and Smith got to the Sports Bar at 6:15 and went in.
Jones has been looking forward to seeing the hypnotist for weeks.	The Sports Bar is in the Good Beer Guide.
The town has 2,234 inhabitants.	

The answer is really quite simple. It is 54. Smith and King go to karate, the coach plus nine players and two reserves go to baseball practice. However, in getting to the answer all sorts of things will happen in the team. They will possibly:

◆ Launch into action and start shouting out what they have on their cards, without planning how to handle the task, demonstrating the need for a conductor to make sure the goal is clear and procedures work.

◆ Ignore the odd comment from someone about how to get the answer.

◆ Demonstrate several examples of falling into the communication trap.

◆ Start to make judgments about what they *assume* is irrelevant information, with no criteria to judge it by.

◆ Agonize over what is *really* irrelevant information, in case they miss something.

◆ Realize after a few minutes that they need a structure, at which point someone will take control and lead the procedures to their logical conclusion.

If your team misses out on any of these points, congratulate them and yourself. These points appear time and again as a common pattern that groups follow. Teams, once they have worked through them, tend to do much better the next time and learn from their mistakes, as long as they have the chance to review what happened.

SUMMARY

The techniques we have looked at in this chapter will help establish some clear procedures for your team. In Chapter 7, we will bring together all the issues we have looked at so far and use them to help your team review where it is and what it needs to do for its own development. If you are unclear about any of the issues or techniques covered so far, go back now and refresh your memory so you are ready for our final chapter.

Chapter 7

We Can Do Better Than This

This chapter brings together all the issues and points we have delved into in the book, and shares them with your team. The first thing we're going to look at is a sort of map, to take you through the initial process of identifying where you are now and where you want to be, clarifying what improvements can be made. Once you have a clear picture, you can take the rest of the team on the same journey, using the same map.

Later in this chapter you will see how important it is, once this initial team building stage has been tackled, to keep an eye on how things are going, so you can make small adjustments that help the team develop further.

AREN'T WE GOOD?

You may be very good, but this question implies complacency and satisfaction with things as they are. A better question is, "How well do we match the quality standard we're aiming for?" The quality standard for teams is the ideal team, operating in the ideal way, and we have spent the last six chapters exploring this.

Unless you believe your team is of perfect quality, there is always room for improvement. If you do believe it couldn't be improved you're either: (a) very lucky; (b) such an effective team leader you didn't need to open this book; or (c) kidding yourself.

Any current management topic—from Total Quality Management to Customer Service to Just-in-Time—has a quality content and depends on teams. The need for an effective team always figures high on the list of essential characteristics. Another point that always appears is that quality implies continuous improvement, rather than a one-shot quick fix; you can always do better!

There is a cycle of questions you need to have answered as you work to improve the quality of your team.

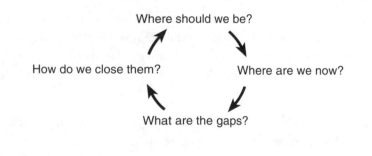

WHERE SHOULD WE BE?

You have started to answer this by the work you have done on:

◆ leadership

◆ goals

◆ team roles

◆ openness and honesty

◆ procedures

What should the team's results be at this point:

This is fairly easy to assess, as long as you built in some objectives that provide a yardstick against which to measure the results. If an objective was

to produce the plan for the garden by the end of August

it's an open-and-shut case. You either did or you didn't. All objectives should have this measurability built in, as you know.

The first task with a team is to focus on its development, while it is still young and impressionable. The emphasis during the rest of this chapter is on the process—the how, rather than the what.

What should the team's process be?

How the team works is hard to quantify, but the impression you now have of what makes a successful team is the best quality standard you can define. It isn't measurable in terms of numbers or product specifications, but it's like what someone once called the elephant test.

It's difficult to describe an elephant, but you know what one looks like and you recognize it when you see it.

The elephant test is good enough. It provides you with a model in your head of what your team would look like if it were doing absolutely everything right every time.

WHERE ARE WE NOW?

This is something you started to look at in Chapter 2, when you completed that short checklist at the end and set some initial priorities. What you did then was take an overall view of all the important characteristics, before you looked at each one in turn.

ACTION POINT

Explain to the team about the overview you looked at in Chapter 2 and give them a copy of the checklist to complete. Accept the fact that, at this stage, they might not be as informed as you are about the details of each characteristic. Just get the broad feel for where everybody thinks the team is now.

87

WHAT ARE THE GAPS?

These show themselves quite plainly. Depending on what sort of scores everybody comes up with, you can assess together where the priorities lie, and these are the biggest gaps.

Naturally, there will be different perceptions throughout the team, so an open discussion is likely to be needed. One reason for very different scores is individuals' unique interpretations of what the words mean, and getting into the detail of each characteristic may be the only way of sorting out any such confusion. So, if there are still very different views, ask people to hold onto them. Explain that they will get the chance to look at the checklist again later, after they have explored what each of the characteristics means.

HOW DO WE CLOSE THE GAPS?

The first step is to check back and make sure that any item on the checklist that looks OK really is OK. Remember, at this stage the team members haven't looked at the openness and honesty issues and so, for instance, they may say you're a brilliant leader because they think that's what they ought to say. You might feel just like one of the team, but if you're the senior person there, the others will always have in the back of their minds that you're the boss.

So ask some probing questions before you decide to accept any issue as being healthy enough to leave for now. Then, once you have identified the most important priority, you as the team leader can relay to the rest of the team what lies behind the issue, using the knowledge you've gained in this book.

If you look back, you'll see that in each chapter you have been asked to do something that you can now ask them to do. The goal has always been to provide you not only with a chance to look at teams yourself, but to establish resources to impart your knowledge and understanding to the rest of the team.

In addition to using the materials you have learned about, there are several other options. They include:

◆ asking the team to come up with solutions and ways to improve themselves

◆ getting a consultant to help you focus on team development

◆ buying one of the many sets of team-building exercises that are on the market

A STARTER FOR 10

It doesn't really matter where you start. So, if you have several priorities you could look at team roles first, because that is a topic that automatically gets everyone involved and starts them talking. Or you may prefer to start with procedures, simply because you have a set of ready-made activities from the previous chapter that you can use.

However, if you start with openness and honesty, you could sort out the ground rules before doing anything else.

There really is no right answer here, just the right answer given your team's situation. What matters is starting somewhere—any-where—rather than getting caught in analysis paralysis and looking for the one right answer that doesn't exist. Go for it!

BACK TO THE BEGINNING

Once you have looked at all the important issues, go back to the original checklist and either get everyone to do it again, or let them see whether they want to reconsider their initial thoughts. This will either confirm or change the top priorities, and ensure that you're devoting your energies to the appropriate areas. It may mean going back and closing any previously hidden gaps, but better to do it now than leave something undone.

KEEPING AN EYE ON THINGS

So, you have taken the first step and worked with the team to look at where it is now and where it wants to be. You have identified the gaps and planned some action to close them.

However, this is only the beginning. Like a child growing up, the team is starting to develop and mature, but it has a long way to go. It still needs attention to detail, so it can keep on developing, rather than staying an adolescent.

DANGEROUS RESULTS

The team starts working and it begins to focus on achieving its goals and objectives. At this point there is the danger that the "what," the results, takes over all the attention from the "how," the process.

Another cycle can help here, because it gives you three simple questions to ask, whenever there is the chance to spend a few minutes reviewing progress.

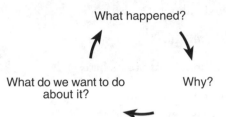

What happened?

What do we want to do about it?

Why?

Asking these simple questions is a process you have seen several times in this book, especially when the notion of someone observing the team and giving feedback appeared. This time, though, the team members themselves ask and answer the questions.

There is a variation you might like to use, by breaking down the "what happened" question into:

◆ What went well?

◆ What went badly?

An example of the answers might look like this. First, something that went badly.

TEAM REVIEW
What went well?

We got the decision sorted out and everybody agrees, even though a couple of us were not originally sold on it.

Why?

Because we accepted we're in this together and it has to be the best possible compromise. We overcame some fairly major differences that would have stopped us in the past.

What do we want to do about it?

Celebrate this success, and do it again next time.

There are a couple of important points here:

◆ Success is worth celebrating because it:
  – confirms things are going well and the team has done the right things;
  – gives people a good feeling;
  – breeds further success.

◆ It is worth reviewing what went well because it clarifies it is something to do again.

TEAM REVIEW

What went badly?

Derek withdrew from the discussion on the timetable.

Why?

Claire and David both snapped at him and wouldn't listen to his point of view. It was getting late by then and we were all a bit tired.

What do we want to do about it?

Alison, as the conductor, needs to jump on situations like that more quickly. Claire and David need to remember the ground rules, so does Derek, who should have been more assertive. Also, we should take a few short breaks so we don't all get so stressed.

Using a simple and short review technique like this will help ensure that all the work you have done is not eroded over time.

And now, the review process when things go well.

Building and maintaining a team is not easy and it doesn't happen on its own, but if you get everyone involved in working out where they want to improve, and how, you will inevitably find you and the other members are part of a successful team, and a very satisfying experience.

SUMMARY

This final chapter brought together all the issues and points that we have looked at throughout this book. Now, the real work begins when you start putting all this into practice. Remember your priorities and don't get distracted.

Finally, reviewing progress and team decisions is the best way to continue making progress.

GLOSSARY

Approach   a particular manner of taking steps to accomplish a particular purpose. *The team's approach to the problem was ineffective.*

Appropriate   especially suitable or compatible. *The team members' action was appropriate in the circumstances.*

Brainstorming   a method of shared problem solving in which all members of a group spontaneously contribute ideas. *All teams would benefit from more brainstorming.*

Collage   an artistic composition of materials and objects pasted over a surface; an assemblage of diverse elements. *In the case of team brainstorming, a collage of paper containing team member ideas may be pasted on the walls of the team meeting room.*

Coordinate   to combine, in harmonious relationship, many parts of an issue or a project. *A team leader will coordinate the efforts of her team.*

Commitment   a binding obligation from an individual to fulfill a promise to another individual or group, such as a team member might make to the rest of the team. *This problem will not be solved without a firm commitment from management.*

Committee   a body of persons delegated to consider, investigate, take action on, or report on some matter; a self-constituted organization for the promotion of a common object. *The team leader appointed a committee to analyze the problem.*

Culture   a set of shared attitudes, values, goals, and practices that characterize a company or a corporation. *Our team must function within the culture of the parent organization.*

Develop   to go through a process of evolution and natural growth by successive changes. *We can develop an effective team only through hard work.*

Effective   producing a decided, decisive, or desired effect. *Effective team members accomplish their assigned tasks in their entirety within budget and time requirements.*

Feedback   transmission of evaluative or corrective information to the original or controlling source about action, event, or process. *A leader may ask for feedback from team members regarding team actions.*

Goal   the end to which effort is directed; an individual or organizational target to be achieved within a particular time period. *An organizational goal may be to become number one in market share of a particular product within the following year.*

Implement   to carry out, accomplish; to give practical effect to and ensure actual fulfillment by concrete measures. *The team leader is responsible for implementing management's requests.*

Initiative   action of creating the energy or aptitude displayed in starting an action. *A team member with initiative possesses the ability to bring forth new ideas or techniques and will take individual action without waiting for instructions.*

Just-in-Time a method of controlling the amount of material and components inventory held in stock to support the production of manufactured goods. *Material and components are delivered to the production line "just in time" to be assembled into the final product.*

Manager person charged with the responsibility of administering and directing an organization's activities. *The manager controls and manipulates resources and expenditures.*

Management key people in an organization. *Those who make the important decisions are known as top management.*

Motivate to create a desire to act with purposeful behavior and to provide oneself or others with a reason to accomplish the desired result. *The project succeeded largely because the leader was able to effectively motivate the team.*

Objective ultimate goal or target of an individual's or group's efforts and strategy. *The team was disbanded when the objective of the project was achieved.*

Perspective The capacity to view things in their true relationships or relative importance; to view one's own task or that of a group within a larger framework. *Each member brought a different perspective to the project.*

Procedure A set of established forms or methods for conducting the affairs of a business. *The nature of the problem dictates the procedure to be followed.*

Process   a series of actions, changes, or functions bringing about a result. *The process of manufacturing a widget is complex.*

Quality   characteristic or standard measure of excellence; a measure of the degree to which something meets a standard. *The team was charged with improving the quality of the work environment.*

Quality control   a system for ensuring the maintenance of proper standards in manufactured goods. *Without quality control, the product would be inferior.*

Relevant   having significant and demonstrable bearing on the matter at hand; information that is available in a timely fashion, before it loses its value in decision making. *Data that provides information about earlier expectations is relevant.*

Scenario   an outline of an expected or a supposed sequence of events. *A scenario is frequently used when planning future projects.*

Specification   a detailed, exact statement of particulars, especially a statement prescribing materials, dimensions, and quality of work for something to be built, installed, or manufactured. *The team was assembled before the specifications for the project were available.*

Strategy   a carefully developed plan of action designed to achieve a particular goal; a complex set of adaptations (as of behavior or structure) that serves an important function in achieving evolutionary success. *The team strategy was to meet frequently for short sessions.*

Team   a number of persons associated together in work or activity; a group organized to work together. *A team was assembled for the purpose of improving the delivery time of large orders.*

Total Quality Management (TQM)   an all-embracing philosophy in which the central focus is continuous quality improvement achieved through organization-wide cooperation, ongoing employee training, and involvement in production or other processes. *All departments of the company demonstrated improved performance after the adoption of Total Quality Management.*

INDEX